CALLING ALL PARENTS - AGAIN

CALLING ALL PARENTS – AGAIN

Leslie H Duncan

The Pentland Press Limited
Edinburgh • Cambridge • Durham • USA

© Leslie H Duncan

ISBN 1 85821 391 6

Published in 1996
by The Pentland Press Ltd.
1 Hutton Close, South Church,
Bishop Auckland, Durham.
Printed and bound by
Lintons Printers,
Crook, Co. Durham.

THE AUTHOR

The name of Leslie Duncan was synonymous with sterling work that he did in Sunday Schools, both at national and local level, down through many years.

He was principal psychologist for the County of Ayr until he retired and was founder of Ayrshire Child Guidance which now covers five main centres.

He was a past president of the Scottish Sunday School Union and until a few years ago was a member of the Executive of the Union and an Elder in Kingcase Church, Prestwick.

In this booklet, Leslie selected the appropriate parts of psychology to explain how problems arise, and how best to deal with them. He brought to his writing a lifetime of experiences from home, school and church.

Leslie Duncan died in January 1995, before the publication of this booklet.

ACKNOWLEDGMENTS

Thanks are due to my daughters, Mrs Petricia Craib and Mrs Eileen Rudolph for checking the script and to my grandchildren, Julie Craib, Kenneth Craib, and Lori Rudolph, for typing the material. Thanks are also due to the Rev. Ian Purves, Kingcase Church Prestwick for permission to include the photo of Kingcase interior and for some of the illustrations in the text. I also wish to thank Eirwen Campbell for her drawings and the Rev. Douglas Aitken for the production of the typeset manuscript.

PREFACE

"The young people of today think of nothing but themselves, they are impatient of all restraint, they talk as if they know everything, and what is wisdom with us is counted foolishness with them. As for the girls, they are forward, immodest and unwomanly in speech, manner and dress."

This was the opinion of Peter the Monk in 1294. A report to parliament in 1818 stated that "the outstanding feature of this dissolute age is juvenile delinquency" which is terrorising the people and destroying their property. It is somewhat reassuring to parents today who may be feeling that Christian nurture is facing a new and difficult task. Children have been difficult in all ages, for parents live in the past but children dwell in the land of tomorrow into which adults cannot enter even in their dreams. A child of 7 years old can operate a video and play computer games as if these were part of everyday life, while word processors and multi-channel satellite TV are familiar to the 12-year-old. Part of the problem is the extent and speed of change but the change is in things not in people. The Concorde is only a very fast camel with wings: an inter-continental missile is still only a faster and more deadly arrow: satellite news is only a faster carrier pigeon. Mankind has not changed. The qualities of love, truth, forgiveness, justice and peace are still in conflict with hatred, lies, revenge, injustice and war; and people must still choose. Unless a child is taught about the need for wise choice at home, school and church, the modern materialistic competitive society is likely to have undue influence on him as he grows up.

In education, great changes are being made, not only in the secular curriculum but also in Religious Education. In our multi-cultured, multi-racial society all religions have to be respected, and teachers must not single out any one religion as superior to the others. "Children," it is said, "must be free to choose for themselves. They must not feel they are being got at." Parents can no longer assume that R.E. in schools means Christian Education as they knew it.

Schools do a different though complementary job. Since, however, Christianity is a "revealed" religion we cannot just leave it to each child to accept or reject it without knowing much about it.

This booklet is intended for Christian parents who as 'People of the Way' seek, in co-operation with school and church, to assist their children in their Faith Quest. Naturally no two families are alike, and thus no general guidance could be given, which could apply to all. What is offered are suggestions from recent research into Christian nurture in the hope that some of the more common problems may be looked at afresh.

SECTION 1

THE PARENTS' ROLE
IN CHRISTIAN NURTURE

In this context, 'nurture' is understood as Christian upbringing, teaching, support, development and encouragement. In marriage, two people who thus far have lived independent lives with their individual likes and dislikes, prejudices and habits, resolve to merge these into one partnership. Considerable re-adjustments are called for and will take time to take effect. One essential factor in this is 'communication'. People who have lived alone for years sometimes go on in their own way regardless of the need for the new partner to be kept informed of what is being planned or where difficulties are being experienced. They must both strive to keep the channels of communication open at all times. Most women can talk over a difficulty — some men clam up and walk away. It is essential to avoid deadlock in family life.

When children come, the situation again calls for considerable readjustment for both mother and father. If the new baby is welcomed and cherished as a gift from God, if they realise that as stewards of a life with infinite potential, their marriage is being enriched, the readjustments will be taken as they come.

What role should they assume as parents? Several models have been suggested.

Firstly, **Mother as Nurse.**

This can be physically demanding as well as emotionally fulfilling. Father is not always so involved and can feel shut out although the new-type father is becoming much more involved in the early nurture partnership.

Secondly, **Parents as Gardeners.**

This is a useful role, for successful growth demands careful preparation of the ground conditions. Most important, however, is the understanding that growth takes time, it cannot be forced. While some shoots may require redirecting, life force is very strong and must be guided rather than repressed.

1

Thirdly, *The Parent Prospector.*

No one can foresee in which form the innate gifts will appear or when they will do so, though mostly they appear in early childhood. Parents should be like prospectors on the lookout for gold, and give every encouragement to the child who has gifts. But while they do so they should also remember that every child has great potential which could be ignored or developed. Even the handicapped child can do more than people think. In the past, some children were classified as ineducable. This is now rejected and even segregation of slow learners is advocated less.

Since there is ability in some form, parents should be prepared to try many interests to see which might prove successful. A parent stated that they had sent their daughter to music, "but it was a complete waste of time and money for she was not willing to practise". This is a wrong view. It was not a waste of money to seek for clues to natural aptitude. Any interest shown has to be tested to see if it indicates future potential ability. The really retarded child could be the genius who has not been recognised or is underachieving for fear of ridicule or estrangement from his classmates.

A fourth model for parents is *Journeying Together.*

This is suggested by Professor John Westerhoff. He thinks of life as a journey in search of faith in which parents and children together learn from each other. It is not what parents do to a child or for a child which is important; it is what they do together with a child. It will be of interest to note that the new programme of the Church of Scotland for Sunday Schools is entitled "Faith Quest" in which home, school and church become partners in learning. For Christian nurture, this model of reciprocal learning is possibly the one for parents to follow.

Whatever the role adopted, parents must respect the uniqueness of the child's own personality. There is no use trying to make him exactly like themselves, much less that they should try to achieve their own lost ambitions through their children.

THE VITAL IMPORTANCE
OF PARENTAL INVOLVEMENT

Advancing in Faith Quest by Imitation of Parents

When a child learns to speak and understand, much of his learning is through imitation. Mother's speech, father's habits, other children's acts tend to be imitated. Even a speech defect can be copied from a brother or sister. In Christian nurture, children are greatly influenced by the attitudes, example and habits of the parents. If parents go to church, if parents pray, children will want to do so also. The same applies unfortunately in the negative. The principle is, "as you do _ _ _ _ so they will do", and so the first gospel that a child reads is the *Acts of the Parents*. For good or ill the foundations of a child's faith are laid in the home. Church and school will carry on the quest in co-operation with parents, but cannot supplant them.

A Great Step Forward Comes At Baptism

When parents present their child for baptism they are called upon to reaffirm their own beliefs and so renew their relationship to God, and in dependence upon God's grace they promise to nurture their child in the Christian way of life through precept and example. (A 'precept' is a moral instruction or rule of action, therefore parents have to make rules and ensure that their children abide by them as they themselves, by example, obey the rules of society.) They are assured from Peter's sermon in Acts 2:39 that the promises of God to professing parents extend also to their children. Both come within the covenant of grace, that totally unmerited gift of God freely offered to all who acknowledge His Kingship. Thereafter, all through the child's life he has access to this grace, "the divine initiative which comes all the way to meet us." (Murdo Ewan MacDonald: *Crisis of Belief*, Epworth Press). All that parents and the church do in Christian upbringing takes place within this all-surrounding movement of grace, providing a constant source of power and guidance to the 'nurture' being experienced. St Paul prayed three times to God to be cured of an illness, and three times he was assured that God's grace was sufficient for him — it was all he would need (2 Corinthians 12:8,9). It is the grace — amazing grace — which comes into a child's life at baptism, and will meet all his needs.

At infant baptism, the congregation stands in token of the fact that they are present as the family of God, pledging themselves to play their part in the Christian upbringing of the child. This family responsibility is vitally important later in welcoming the child to worship, and later still in the fellowship of the Table at Communion. It is also reassuring to the parents who are naturally concerned about their ability to fulfil their promises of 'nurture'. They can be assured that Christian development is not initiated by themselves alone, but that parents and congregation together are pledging themselves to co-operate with God's initiative for their child through His grace. Mistakes inevitably will be made from time to time by all parents, but since the all surrounding grace is ever present, God's demand is not for perfection, but for faithfulness to the high calling of working with Him.

Jesus' Attitude to Children

Some parents fail to understand the place that Jesus gave to children. In the gospels we read that He took a little child and placed him in the midst of the disciples and said, "Whoever welcomes this child in my name, welcomes me." This was a startling statement, for in those days children had no significance. In the synagogue they were segregated along with the women, often behind a screen — they could observe the worship but took no part in it. Again, when the mothers of Jesus' time brought their children to Jesus that He might bless them, the disciples attempted to drive them away. Jesus was greatly displeased. He rebuked them and said, "Let the children come to me and do not stop them because the Kingdom of God belongs to such as these." Note that Jesus says, "belongs," not, "will belong," when they grow up or when they will understand or when they join the church. The word of Jesus is that the reign of God is clearly exercised among children. They can call Him Abba — Father — in trust and love.

SECTION 2

SOME GENERAL GUIDELINES ON 'NURTURE'

A. Know Your Child

Two forces combine in the development of a child: heredity factors which are innate or inborn, and environmental factors which are acquired or learned by education. From one's heredity come such gifts as intelligence and special aptitude skills such as music, art, scientific or mathematical ability. These special gifts show early in life, e.g. Mozart could pick out chords for himself at the age of three, and at five he began composing small pieces which were published when he was seven. Recently, a boy of nine years of age sat the A level mathematics paper.

Behaviour is learned from the Family Pattern, and since no two families are alike, behaviour can be very diverse. Both heredity and environment are essential for development. The boy of nine had a father who taught him mathematics, but the innate gift was first there, for not all maths teachers have sons who are at A level at age nine. A good heredity tends to show up in spite of environmental weakness, though on a smaller scale. Someone with the inherited gifts of a Beethoven, if born in the jungle, would not compose the Ninth Symphony, but the gifts would show up in the jungle environment, and he would likely become the best tom-tom beater for miles around.

B. Growth Takes Time

Time is an essential element in the growth of a child. Why it takes a certain time for certain functions to mature is unknown, but there is a definite time factor which cannot be disregarded. "Man's lessons are usually premature." By adults, childhood seems often to be regarded as a blunder which has to be hurried over as quickly as possible. The most common question parents ask is, "When should he be able to do _ _ _ _ ?" The second is, "Mrs. Smith's boy is the same age as my son, but he can do _ _ _ _ and my son cannot." There is no set age for development to show. A child will walk when

6

his mind and body co-ordination is ready for it; he will not wet the bed at night when he is ready. One thing is sure, however: undue anxiety by the parent will tend to cause anxiety in the child, and undermine the self-image which is being built up. Scolding, ridicule and punishment in such a case are recessive, but loving support, praise in any success and approval of trying, are all stimuli to stability and growth. There is indeed possible harm in trying to force progress, for an emotional shock can cause the child to regress to the very level that the parent had been so proud to boast that he had achieved. A parent who insisted on very correct speech in advance of others in the class, found her son developed a speech disorder following a fright with a dog. So too, toilet training achieved too quickly can create an anxiety and fear of failure which can be lasting. Unfortunately, disappointed by the return to, say, wetting or soiling, the parent may tend to react emotionally, moving from one 'treatment' to another, without giving any one of them time to take effect, and lowering his self-esteem by calling him a baby, and threatening to put him back in nappies.

If some development is about two years behind the child's peer-group, the situation could be reviewed. The first step would be to consult a doctor to check if there is any physical cause. If none is found, the psychologist could check for possible retardation. Both having cleared the position, two things can be done. Encourage self-help rather than depend on others to do it for him. Jesus' method was often to put the onus on the patient. "Do you want to be healed?" "Rise up, and walk." To promote this self-help, the child could keep a record of progress, for knowledge of obvious success or improvement is a great incentive to learning. A simple reward for success may be useful, though praise is better than material gifts. Why? The child is tempted to demand a reward and may even try to increase it as time goes on. It could be that the parent has shown too great anxiety which a clever child could exploit, and so parents should keep the responsibility for cure firmly on the child. Parents tend to feel responsible for their child longer than necessary. When a Jewish boy becomes 'adult' at thirteen, as part of the Bar Mitzvah ceremony the father thanks God that he is no longer responsible for his son's future conduct. Thereafter, both know where they stand. It might be salutary if adolescents could hear this prayer on their behalf in their late teens.

Certain adults and certain children seem to enjoy collecting 'scalps' like the Red Indians of the past. "I've been to four specialists and not one of them could cure me!" Jesus' question is still relevant: "*Do you* want to be healed?"

C. The Importance Of Praise

There is a saying, "Nothing succeeds like success", and this is a very strong incentive in all walks of life. A child soon tires of a game or study in which he is hopelessly beaten every time he tries. Success does encourage, and so in school, marks, stars, prizes and medals are used to indicate to all that success has been achieved. In the home, these are not so valuable, but of all incentives, praise is the most important.

Some parents tend to believe that criticism will keep the child from taking things too easy, and that it will spur him on to greater effort. This is not necessarily so. Praise, on the other hand, is positive, like sunshine to the growing plant, and indicates that the parent has confidence in the child's ability to succeed. The family pattern is to reassure, even though the child may not be sure if it is going to work. Being silent is worse than not trying an answer. In most questions, there is usually more than one possible solution, and so they praise the effort, and show the correct way.

"Am I being good now?"

D. The Family Pattern

For the sake of order in the home, each family works to a pattern of behaviour which suits the particular circumstances. A one-parent family, a broken home family, a family from the East, a family with father unemployed, will all work out an appropriate pattern. There is no ideal family or correct pattern that others should imitate, for children growing up in the family learn the behaviour patterns of the parents. Children are programmed in behaviour. Accordingly, parents should strive to ensure that the pattern they adopt is understood and followed, for this gives stability — each one knows where he stands and that he has his place in it. On occasion, people try to look for the causes of misbehaviour in the parents' family background: his brother or uncle or aunt was a problem, but behaviour is learned. It is not so much that he is a chip off the old block; it is living with the old block that does the damage.

While the provision of a dependable routine lays the foundations of security, each program must be structured to meet the changing development of the living and growing family. There is a tendency for a routine, once successful, to persist long after its 'use by date' has passed. In everyday life, there are numerous relics of obsolete practices and phrases. One hint that there is a need to consider a change, is when anger or opposition rises, especially if it is unexpected or 'out of the blue'.

With a young child it is usually easy to lay down a rule of law in the home and outside, but it must be programmed in a way of becoming socially adjusted. There will always be a tendency to test out the power of the parental control, especially in the present climate of self-direction. Parents have been subjected to 'modernistic' blackmail. The child's defence, "You are not allowed to smack me now," has been allowed to become the accepted philosophy, thereby removing one of the past methods of discipline without substituting any alternative control. The change has come so quickly that children have had no opportunity to grow into the new ideas. The art of being a 'good parent' lies in the ability to keep a close eye on what is vital and basic to the welfare of the child in his growth to respon-sibility and social adjustment in a family.

One solution is to develop the idea of a family conference to teach the importance of a group decision which takes into account all the members' differing points of view. "Not fair," is a common family complaint at home and in school which has to be redirected rather than ignored.

A mother who had unwittingly favoured the boys in a family rather than the girls said to one of her daughters, "Run and get Ian's slippers." This had happened on other occasions with little objection but the injustice of the demand surfaced on this occasion and the daughter replied, " Why should I ? Let him get his own slippers."

Such a response should make parents pause to consider possible injustices previously overlooked, rather than an expression of disobedience. After a brief pause, the mother replied, "Quite right! I had not thought of it in that way before." The positive reaction to a routine no longer useful is valuable to the family pattern. In general, any routine must be capable of review.

The 'Family Pattern' is vital in establishing 'Family Laws' which parents must establish in the early years.

1. They make it clear that, when in someone's house, they must not take away a toy or anything which is attractive, without first asking permission to do so.

2. 'Finders Keepers' is not the way to behave. If they find something of value, they must not keep it until they ask mother or a teacher if they may keep it.

3. In a shop or supermarket, they will see shoppers filling their baskets and they may be tempted to do so also. Parents must not be remiss in warning about stealing. At the check-out counter, there is often a sweet point. This is a situation to be watched.

E. The Importance Of Manners In Christian 'Nurture' In The Home

In former times children were taught to be polite, to say please and thank you, etc. These social graces tend to be forgotten, yet they are basic in Christian nurture. When a child asks for something, he is encouraged to say "please". If he does not say this to his parents, whom he is seeing, how is he to be taught to say "please" to God whom he has not seen? The same problem comes in saying "sorry". It is sometimes not easy to admit a mistake and to say sorry, but it is important, for repentance is a relevant element in prayer and should be programmed in the early years.

Thanksgiving, too, has a home training element. Children tend to omit it, and parents get tired of demanding good manners. Yet how can a child come to thank God, if that is not part of the family pattern?

On occasion, parents put on a show of manners to impress visitors. This is bad psychology, for false manners usually fail; but also the parents are programming their children to deceive the very person that they hoped to please. The minister has called and has accepted the offer of a cup of tea. Mother passes the biscuits to her son and asks, "Would you like another?" Answer: "NO!" To save the situation, mother says in her two-edged voice, "No what, dear?" Answer: "No way!"

If the unwanted behaviour does not improve, the cause may be in one of the following ways.

1. **Objective** — The correct way may not have been clearly stated, or his friends do the opposite and he wants to copy them.

2. **Teaching** — The parent may not be providing a consistent example, e.g. a young person will not feel that smoking is undesirable if one of the parents smokes or admired relatives do so. Most likely, however, the parents have overlooked a failure to comply. Some children tend to test out a command to see if the parents really mean what they say. When asking for something to be done, make sure that it is being done. If asking for something to stop, teach that your

red light says stop and means stop. For example, mother and child are shopping, and mother is in conversation with the assistant, while the child is going around touching things. Mother notices this and says, "Stop touching those tins," but then goes on with the conversation. She turns and says, "Now that's the last time I'll tell you to stop touching those tins," but again turns round to the assistant. Finally, the pile of tins is knocked over and mother turns to the onlookers and remarks, "What do you know! I told him to stop it."

What should she have done? Having told the child once to stop touching, mother waits to make sure that the child has done so. If he persists, mother goes over to the child, takes him by the hand and says, "Stand beside me, till I have finished talking."

Parents will recall a teacher who would say, "How many times have I to tell you to be quiet and get on with your work?" Having told the class once with no effect, it is useless to repeat it. Action must follow a command.

3. **Consequences**   Penalty must be imposed by the person involved otherwise the same thing will happen again. Waiting till father gets home may suit in some families, but if father is at sea or if there is no father, mother learns to handle the situation, and only she who knows the family setting, can devise the family penalty. Penalties depend on the child. To one, sending him to bed would be no penalty at all. One useful penalty is 'time-out' i.e. exclusion from the group with a given time limit (as in sport a three minute time-out from the field of play). The fixed time ensures that the child's interest is maintained, and, as he is usually keen to get back to the group, the penalty is effective.

4. **Emotional Blackmail Should Be Resisted** — "*Give me or else!*" Children, on occasion, discover that parents can be bullied. A single parent is especially vulnerable. If, therefore, a child threatens "Give me or else I'll _ _ _ _ ," it must be the 'or else'. Appeasement in life, as in history, solves nothing. A parent offered to give a child 5p if he would say his prayers each night. She soon realised that this

was ineffective when he later demanded 10p.

"If you give me _ _ _ _ I'll go to school." Here again, the child feels that he is in command of the situation and there will be no end to the demands. The child who succeeds in blackmail will grow up to be very difficult to live with as an adult, and will tend to develop a pattern of aggression to any thwarting of his own desires.

**"Give me —
or else ...!"**

5. **The Three Step Caution For Very Young Children** With a young child about to do something undesirable or dangerous, parents can take three simple steps meaning stop; *a look, a sign, a word.*

A Look - When a child seems likely to be in danger or to do something undesirable, look at the child and get eye contact. This is an important stop signal, for this is an innate method of communication which is very effective as a first step. Teachers are accustomed to this method, and even animals can react to it. There is no need to shout.

A Sign - A raised hand indicating stop, or a finger pointing, conveys the same message. The sign should be clear and definite, as when the referee points to the dressing room in ordering off a player.

A Word - It may be necessary to use a word. It could be the cautionary, "ah-ah!" or, "Now then!" or the child's name, "John!" A child who had been cautioned by the 'ah-ah!' method, was later heard to say it to the baby brother. When the mother asked, "Where did you learn that?" she replied, "That's what Grandpa says!"

Naturally, if a child has been conditioned to be shouted at, he may not respond at first. In such a case, mother should walk over quietly and lead the child to where the behaviour can be controlled. Clear action without anger or fuss helps to prevent emotional counter-reaction, for emotion in the child is often generated by emotion in the mother. But what if this causes a scene? Parents sometimes give in for the sake of peace. There will be no peace, and demands will only increase if children (and indeed adults) find that a scene will pay off. Children have to discover from experience that a wild outburst will achieve nothing.

6. **Bad Behaviour Learned Outside** — Inevitably, a child may hear others using bad language, and try it at home to see what parents will do about it. It will be very satisfying to the child if parents express shock: that is what he had hoped would be the effect. Parents should 'appear' to be unmoved, but should stress, "We do not use that language in this house." If the words are repeated, a suitable family penalty follows.

When a child goes wrong, it is not so much that he has been taught bad habits. Most times it is because he has been left without clear guidance. Here Christian nurture has a part to play in setting out the difference between right and wrong. For young children, parents should set clear boundaries, which can be imprinted in behaviour.

About Rewards — A reward should be regarded as a sign of approval for improvement not automatically given for anything done. Material reward is less useful than praise, a story, a special treat, e.g. a picnic or a visit to some place where the child really wanted to go.

F. Learning By Asking Questions
It has been noticed how the child learns the meaning of things

and of people in the world in which he lives by imitation and by repetition of experience. An important new means of learning is opened up when he learns to speak and ask questions: "Who?" and "What?" seek to get information about people and things, "How?" and "Why?" seek to get information about causes and reasons. Questions can become a source of irritation to parents and teachers but it must be remembered that this is the child's natural method of learning. As Kipling says:

> *I keep six honest serving-men*
> *(They taught me all I know);*
> *Their names are What?, and Why?, and When?*
> *And How?, and Where?, and Who?*

Questions, therefore, are the growing points which should be aroused and stimulated so that when the child grows older he will have developed this method of learning and made it habitual.

Encourage Self Teaching, By Giving Insight Into The General Pattern
— If the child can easily find out the answer for himself, encourage him to do so by showing the general method: e.g., "Where is Nazareth?" is answered by showing how to find where Nazareth, and any other place, is. Thus, the one answer disposes once and for all of any later questions of similar type. Again, showing how to use a dictionary answers how to spell words, and a concordance gives the key to the place of any Bible quotation. The knowledge, instead of being an isolated fact, becomes a basic pattern for use in all future problems of a similar nature. (This is the modern method of child-centred learning.)

In some homes, parents are very busy about the house and may feel that a child's stream of questions is very time-consuming, and tell him to go and play, read a book or watch TV. This can be quite a discouragement to asking further questions.

On the spur of the moment, a parent may give the first answer that comes to mind and it may be incorrect. The child may conclude that parents are not interested in him, and if the answer turns out to be incorrect, the child's dependence on getting correct answers is endangered.

If, therefore, the parent does not know the answer, avoid postponing the answer, admit that you do not know, but add, "**We'll** find out the answers from someone who knows these things." This has three lessons in the art of learning.

- It teaches that it is not wrong not to know, so long as you try to find the answer.

- It encourages both child and parent to co-operate in the quest.

- It reduces the barrier of youth and age when the child discovers that parents do not know everything.

A child's attempt to gain attention can cause him to keep on asking. Indeed, while the parent is answering, the child is thinking of the next one that he can ask. If this is becoming a habit, seek to discover why he seeks attention in this way. Is he testing the answers or testing the parent? It may be merely a device to postpone being sent to bed, or being questioned himself.

SECTION 3

CHILD DEVELOPMENT

ASPECTS OF DEVELOPMENT

There are many aspects of development. Some of these are physical, mental, emotional, social, creational, moral and spiritual. For convenience, each can be studied separately, but we must never forget the unique oneness — the unity of development. More and more, the principle of wholeness in medicine and education is being recognised. Weakness in any one of the aspects tends to have an effect on all the others. Poor physical development can affect the social and emotional development, as well as the well-known effect on the mental development. The build-up of the very important element of self-esteem is affected by any weak aspect, and loss of confidence is often the result.

1. Physical Development

At birth, the cells regulating physical development are complete, and the body has only to feed and grow through appropriate exercise. The equipment of the play centre is specially selected to ensure the proper development, first of the large muscles, and later of the smaller ones of fingers and tongue. One of the best means of physical development is through swimming. Apart from the exercise, swimming greatly enhances self-image and confidence. Water is a natural element, and the conquest of water is very rewarding. Physical development is important because conscious control of the body is the first stage of conscious control of the mind. The ancient Greeks spent half the school time in the academy and half the time in the gymnasium. A healthy mind in a healthy body was their aim, once more showing the importance of all elements of development.

2. Mental Development

Though the cells regulating physical development are complete at birth, the brain cells have still to be formed into language systems. The cells, however, multiply rapidly. By the age of about 4, 40% of the framework is complete, and the child going to school has learned as much as he will do in the next five years of schooling. Language seems to be partly innate and partly due to learning. The child learns to speak by listening to words and speaking words taught by mother and teacher, but recent research has shown that the grammatical rules of language are somehow innate. The child who says, "I doed it" or "I seed it" is applying a standard grammatical rule in a perfectly logical manner. Unfortunately, English grammar is not perfectly logical. The maturing integrative mind seems to be able to organise words independently of any teaching.

Learning With Understanding

Incoming information about the world passes to the brain via the various senses, especially that of sight. "A picture is worth a thousand words." The assimilative nature of the brain joins up like material to form what might be called a 'data-bank' of interest centres. If incoming material is carefully prepared and organised, the brain can classify it correctly. If, however, it is jumbled up and uncertain, learning is hindered. It is important therefore, that any material to be learned is clearly understood. Learning with understanding is six times as fast and ten times more lasting than 'parrot memory.'

Children are usually anxious to please, and will endeavour to learn material in school even if it is not understood. Having no interest centre to which the new material can be assigned, it is liable to go into what might be called a 'junk-box.' A great deal of material 'learned up' for examination purposes is later assigned to the 'box' once the exams are over. One danger of trying to memorize material before understanding it, is that if a child (or adult) memorizes material without understanding it, he is liable to believe that he understands it because he can repeat it. This has important lessons for Religious Education, e.g. if the Lord's Prayer is taught as the Family Prayer before it can be understood, it can become a meaningless ritual which makes future understanding difficult.

3. Social Development

Jesus gave us two commandments: "Love God and your neighbour." In Christian nurture, therefore, encourage social development.

If a child is to live on a deserted island, a life of seclusion would provide no problem, but he has to come out of the self-centred phase of early life to learn right relationships with others. Up to about age 3, he is not particularly interested in other people, except to demand attention. 'Only children' especially are apt to live in a fantasy world of their own. Half the time in a playgroup could be spent quite happily in solitary play. The same applies to children brought up in remote areas of the country. Left to himself to make his own fantasy world, he could tend to lose contact with reality. By the age of about 3, therefore, if he is not showing interest in others, he should be encouraged to do so by mixing with others in a playgroup and nursery Sunday school.

The Value And Importance Of The Church Playgroup And Crèche

In former days of larger families, social development was easy to ensure in the home. The modern one/two child family makes this difficult. Moreover, the modern house has no room for large play equipment or space for running about, and is too tidy to suffer the use of paints, crayons and creative play materials. Equally important, families were closer together and could offer support and advice to young mothers with the usual family problems. *Mother and Toddler groups* are important church back-up provision; most churches have ample space during the day and members of the congregation can offer their assistance. *The Crèche* is also important, especially on a Sunday, to enable parents of small children to maintain their regular attendance at church. Christian Parenting is based on the Christian Home Pattern. It is all too easy to lose church contact in the child's early years and difficult to re-establish it later. *The Playgroup*. At first, most children want to seize all the toys. If anyone is riding on a tricycle, someone will want it too, and try to get it by the three infant responses — force, temper or sulking. Home experience will have programmed him as to which is most effective in getting what he wants. In the playgroup, the rule is that each child counts for one, but not more than one, and no one is permitted to take away a toy from another child. He must learn to wait until the rider is finished with it.

Interest, however, is very fleeting, and a child will abandon a series of toys, leaving them strewn around. Playgroup motto is that each child puts away the toy after using it before taking out another one. 'Helpers' can begin programming each child to see others as well as himself by suggesting sharing: "Let Hazel have a ride on *the* cycle." (Not on *your* cycle.)

The Problem Child In The Playgroup

On occasion, the leader of the Group may be faced with a problem child — generally a boy — who runs about the room, upsetting the toys and causing such distress to the younger ones that their mothers stop bringing them to the playgroup. The first reaction may be to exclude him, but the Church family deals with it within the family group.

1. Allocate a helper to take a personal interest in the boy, and discuss a planned programme with the mother and minister.

2. Since destructiveness is unlived or unused energy, it should be redirected rather than merely repressed. The strength of character which often underlies the 'rebel' is too valuable to neglect.

3. Keep the parents fully informed of your retraining programme.

Programme

a. Provide adequate *physical* activity: ring games, marching, toy bikes.

b. Provide adequate *quiet* activity: jigsaws, books.

c. Provide adequate *creative* activity: paints, clay, Lego.

d. Provide adequate *control,* by imposing a 'time-out' system of control.

e. Provide adequate *social* activity: ring games, singing games.

f. Provide record of progress for helper, mother and child.

g. Develop a warm personal relationship by home visits and cards at birthdays etc.

h. Develop infinite patience. Remember Jesus' words: "I will never turn away anyone who comes to me." (John 6:37).

i. Praise any success.

j. If all fails, seek professional help.

SECTION 4

THE IMPORTANCE OF THE EARLY YEARS

Laying The Foundations Of Faith

Christian nurture is built on the early experience of love and stability of a Christian home. At first, the child is not aware of any Christian teaching as such, but at feed time he experiences the warmth of his mother, and can react to her touch at bath-time. In both activities, the mother is conveying through touch far more than food or bathing. The loving care being experienced is satisfying and reassuring. Any impatience, any hurry, any anxiety is also being conveyed, for these dictate how the child will be held by the mother. If the child is placid and accepting, mother tends to relax, and feeding and bathing are easy and pleasurable. If, however, the child does not want to feed or be bathed, mother's emotion tends to boil up — unfortunately often on small grounds, and tension follows with remarkable build-up. The uncertainty of a mother as to what to do, increases the emotional battle.

Though the child has become emotional there is no need for mother to go into battle as well. If mother can relax, the child will tend to do so also. Parents should endeavour to avoid an emotional battle if possible. The child can keep it up all day if necessary, and can even make himself sick in revenge if, for example, forced to eat something. The difficulty is that when a battle arises, both child's and mother's emotions are aroused to such an extent, that neither reacts normally.

A young child is very self-centred. Everything seems to revolve round him, and family and friends minister to his every call. Left unguided, he would become quite difficult in a normal family, and he has to learn that each counts as one in the family, but not more than one. This social development seems to appear about the age of four years. By playing with other children, he discovers that he can build better sand castles or find greater satisfaction in working and playing, and hence live with others, pave the way to his need to go out to school, and leave the family security. Children in remote areas or deprived of social contacts find the move to the outside world of the school highly disturbing, and school refusal can occur.

The question is, will he go forward or remain at the dependent level? Every child is programmed by his home and his experience outside the home to take a positive, neutral or negative attitude to life. "Who am I? Am I someone loved and supported? Am I someone who has certain personal possessions which no one takes away? Have I some special ability which is encouraged and developed, or am I unloved and abandoned, with no real place in the family? Am I allowed to drift without guidance or correction?"

Educational research has shown that the first five years almost determine the child's attitude to life. There is an innate fight for survival: even among the destitute and starving the will to live is present, but neglect and starvation can often make a child apathetic and listless. At this stage, the presence and influence of a loving family can provide the secure base-camp from which the child can move fearlessly into the unknown, secure in the knowledge that the base-camp is sure and steadfast, and from it he can conquer the world.

A Code Of Behaviour For Our Young People
In Paul's letter to the Philippians (chapter 4:8) he sets down a code of behaviour for our young people of the church, "fill your minds with those things that are good and that deserve praise: things that are true, noble, right, pure, lovely and honourable."

SECTION 5

ESSENTIALS OF CHRISTIAN NURTURE 1

God Is Creator

The first books of the old and the new testament begin with the basic truth about God. He is the Creator, the Maker of all things. "Through him all things came to be, no single thing was created without him." (John 1:3.)

Young children absorb the truth that God is the Maker by seeing the beauty of field and garden, by watching the changing seasons. A child experiencing these with his mother naturally asks, "Who made the flowers grow?" The experience of helping in the garden can open up vital opportunities ·to learn that God is the Creator of all things. Having experienced them in real life, he is ready for the lesson of God as Maker.

God Is Love

Experience comes before instruction, and experience of being loved is the first step in Christian nurture. Christian love, however, is love plus. Ordinary love is as old as life itself. It begins with the Creator God, who is the origin of life and love. It is portrayed throughout the Old Testament. Especially in the Psalms and in the life experiences of Hosea, it was obvious that God loves, but love in the Old Testament was incomplete. With the birth of Jesus, love took on a totally new dimension.

To some extent parents fail to understand that Christmas with its coloured lights and candles, its Christmas tree, its parties and presents, actually celebrates the 'Incarnation' — the greatest event in world history — the revelation of love divine, all loves excelling. No prophet in the Old Testament would have stated that, "love came down at Christmas," or that, "the Word became a human being and full of grace and truth, lived among us." (John 1:4.)

This new depth of love is well described by St. Paul in 1 Corinthians 13. Parents are probably familiar with the passage for it is often read in church, but it's very familiarity may make it less striking. It is all too easy in the silence of the service, sitting among friends and away from the daily chores to agree that "love is patient, love is kind, there is nothing love cannot face." The chapter ends with the general statement, "the greatest of them is love." Most readers stop there and thus ignore the three practical words of Paul's message. These occur in the next chapter. "Put love first," (N.E.B.) or, "It is love then that you should strive for." (G.N.B.) 1 Corinthians 14:1. Do we indeed put love first?

Love Experience Has To Be Reinforced

The experience of being loved and of seeing love in action has to be reinforced in the day-to-day routine of the family, for many incidents will occur which will cause the child to wonder if he is really loved. Do parents really love other people? Are the parents really seeing God in the handicapped, the unlovable, the unacceptable? Again, when he is reprimanded or punished, is he still loved? He wonders if love depends on being 'good'. Gradually, and only after repeated experience of the steadfastness of this love, the child comes to understand the significance of being loved, and thence comes the desire to love in return. At first, his love is a selfish type of love, in his growing sense of his power he wants to manipulate things and people to the n'th degree, but the parents' example of love is patient and forward-looking, and by their own unselfish love they teach that love is unconditional — it gives, rather than demands the response of being good, and gives back love in return. Love never changes, it is sure and steadfast.

One way of enabling a self-centred, demanding child to open

out, is through a favourite doll or teddy. These provide an emotional outlet which is not personal, and yet is living, in their eyes. When in trouble, the child can tell Teddy all his difficulties — Teddy understands and supports. Later, when the child is learning to show concern for others, a live pet gives a link between child and real people. It is not easy, yet this love should enable us in time to love our enemies. Jesus showed the way when on the cross He could still pray, "Forgive them, Father! They don't know what they are doing." (Luke 23:34.) It is not an easy religion, but since God came down and dwelt among us, since He involves Himself in our affairs, we must strive to recognise Him in all creation. George MacLeod in one of his prayers puts it thus:

"With earthly eyes we see men and women: tall or short: exuberant or dull but with the eyes of faith, we know you dwell in each."

Mother Theresa's daily prayer expresses the same insight:

"Dearest Lord, may I see you today and every day, in the person of your sick and whilst nursing them, minister unto you. Though you hide yourself behind the unattractive disguise of the irritable, the exacting, the unreasonable, may I still recognise you."

Jesus had the same thought when he said:

"Anything you did for one of my brothers here, however humble, you did it for me." (N.E.B.) Matthew 25:40.

It is the great challenge to parents to seek to see their children and others with the eye of faith, and then help them also to see God in those they meet: the clever and lovable but also the handicapped and the rejected. Professor Barclay says:

"Christian love is not simply a response of the heart that goes out to others; it is our whole personality. You must try never to wish anything but

26

good for others. You must try to look at every man with the eyes of God, with the eyes of goodwill."

In Romans 8:28, Paul puts it thus:

"All things work together for good." (A.V.)

This does not mean that we need not be concerned for the present, for all will come out right in the end. Christian faith faces up to reality. Sorrow is still sorrow, suffering is still suffering, evil is still evil, but the New English Bible translation of the message is more helpful: *"In all things God co-operates for good with those who love him."*

He co-operates here and now as well as in the future. Thus, a positive attitude to life depending on grace is absorbed daily from the home events, as interpreted by the parents. Because they believe and trust in the divine providence, the child learns to reply to any situation in belief and trust. It has been said that spiritual nurture is caught as well as taught. Much more true, it has also to be lived.

ESSENTIALS OF CHRISTIAN NURTURE 2

Forgiveness And Acceptance

A child learns about forgiveness by being forgiven many times before he can understand what it involves. In the complex activity of life, mistakes are bound to occur, but these can be regarded as ways of learning not to make the same mistake twice. A child should discover by experience that, if he is truly sorry, he will be accepted and forgiven, no matter what he has done, or how unacceptable he may feel.

By being forgiven at home, a child can come to understand how God can also forgive — the relationship which was broken by the wrong-doing is restored. On occasion, a penalty may be imposed which is as near to the offence as possible, e.g. spilling something involves wiping it up, omitting to do a chore involves going back and doing it, breaking a window deliberately involves trying to pay for it. Once a penalty has been paid, the matter is over and done with. "Love does not keep a record of wrongs." (1 Corinthians 13:5.) The truth that God is a loving, understanding, forgiving father develops from the experience of loving, forgiving parents, and later from the experiences in church life of loving, forgiving Christian people.

ESSENTIALS OF CHRISTIAN NURTURE 3

Importance Of Truth

Jesus says in John 8:14, "What I say is true." This is the authority which justifies Christian nurture, otherwise all further efforts are in vain. It is necessary, however, to nurture truth for family use, but especially for assurance in Christian thinking. On occasion someone may say, "This child is a born liar." This is not so. Telling the truth is not innate (inborn), it is learned. Self-preservation is a child's first reaction in trouble. A headmaster once said, "Even if you catch them red-handed, they will deny it black." Teachers and parents have long ago learned this.

Truth is a learned response which has to be programmed through repeated Christian experience and repeated deliberate training. While the young child is learning, mistakes will be made, but love is patient, is not easily provoked, and gradually the family pattern is absorbed and practised. The child tends to tell a lie to avoid reprimand or punishment. It is the task of the parent to show the importance of truth. "If you are in trouble we will help you but we cannot do so if we do not know the facts." A child has to learn, after several experiences, that parents will help. He has also to be assured that the parent will understand and that he will be accepted and forgiven, if he is sorry and will try to do better next time. Parents can show how telling a lie only leads to further lies, and to avoid this they should not lead a child on to add one lie to another. If the parent knows that the child is telling a lie, they should patiently repeat the question, e.g. "Where were you?" in a manner which tells the child only too plainly that his story is not believed. Sometimes the parent is not sure if the story is true. In this case, they should check first if possible before jumping to conclusions. Children have to learn that they are trusted and that they can trust their parents.

The family pattern of truth may take some time to establish.

One common situation is when a child steals some money. This usually occurs first in the home. The child wants to buy something and parents can be remiss in this matter. They may tell the child, "You'll get it in my purse!" They may leave loose change lying about. They may even tell the child their cash card number. They may have stopped his pocket money just when he had arranged to go out with friends.

All these situations set a problem for the child - there is a conflict of loyalties, and there may be the fact that he got away with it in the past. One answer is to make it clear that you know and will be checking on it in future. Above all, do so, for the child will almost inevitably try it out to see if you mean what you say. It may be that the parents' attitude to money has been slack, and the parents' attitude to theft in business or trade may militate against honesty in general. In all situations of dishonesty, check your home pattern.

The family pattern is one element in the training, but a powerful counter to home training could be the negative influence of the outside world pattern. A child cannot be isolated from this influence, and therefore has to be programmed in advance. "What your friends do does not make it right. In our family we _ _ _ _." Clear direction must be given. It does not guarantee that the child will follow it, but he will be in no doubt as to what the parents will approve. Being loving and understanding does not mean being vague or uncertain about basic beliefs.

Children sometimes are excused for wrong-doing by saying, "He is easily led." If he is, why is he easily led astray and not easily led in the right direction? His home training has been lacking in clear direction of the family pattern of accepted behaviour. For wrong habits to triumph, it is only necessary for parents to do nothing. In modern times, drug addiction, alcohol abuse, sexual deviation, must not be left to work away unnoticed and unchallenged.

The Conquest Of Fear

The Battle of the Fears goes on all through early childhood, and these fears must be conquered early lest, all their days, children will be controlled by them. There are few specific innate fears - they are not afraid of animals, fire, water, heights - but these and other fears can be learned from other people, or by association with an unpleasant incident, e.g. being involved in an accident, being bitten, burned, lost or harmed by a stranger.

The danger of fear is that it spreads rapidly to other linked subjects in association, though initially these were harmless. A road accident can lead to fear of hospital, or to doctors in white coats, then widening to anyone in a white coat, and so on.

In playgroups, some common fear situations are acted as play e.g. going to hospital, being examined by the doctor and using 'pretend' bandages, stethoscopes and face masks, enable the children to get used to them in a group situation. Given time to prepare and given support in the event, most children can learn to cope with fear.

Since many fears are learned, they can also be unlearned, by beginning in small ways to face, with support, what is feared. Jesus taught by his own example to face up to the problem. Remember John's words, "Perfect love drives out all fear." (1 John 4:18.)

A child says, "There is a bogeyman, (or some other object of fear) upstairs." It is no use telling a child there is nothing upstairs, to him there is something. Telling him not to be a baby only reduces his confidence further. Say, "Let's go upstairs together. We'll take a torch and stick and we'll soon sort him out." Praise him if he agrees to go. "Good lad, you are well able to tackle this _ _ _ _." The child discovers by experience that fears can be faced. The old proverb, "He who fights and runs away has to fight another day," is true, we have to face up to fears. There is no escape in life situations, they only come again with greater force.

Getting lost in town is a common situation. Before going shopping therefore say, "If you miss me, stand where you are and call out. I'll soon find you." Notice avoid saying, "If you get lost," or, "Try to find me."

Jesus was very much aware of the effect of fear. Again and again, he urges, "Don't be afraid, only believe." (Mark 5:36.) Parents can do much to teach their children how to cope with a fear situation. It is often associated with loss of some kind — a favourite toy, a loved pet, a loved relative. Remember, it is not loss, but sudden unexpected loss which does the damage. If any loss is expected, parents should prepare in advance.

A child has no memory bank of experience of loss, and so he has to rely on parents to guide him how to react. If the parents show control of emotion, their calmness will evoke a similar calmness in the child. Panic and despair by adults runs like wildfire through a group hitherto unmoved.

Certain situations which could cause fear can be anticipated, and appropriate action practised, e.g. bleeding (teach to hold the place with a handkerchief and get help); drowning (teach to swim as early as possible, and certainly before age 6 or 7); going with strangers (teach to say "No"). Each family will have their own particular situations and will teach how to act.

In older children, it may help to explain that emotion was useful in past ages to stimulate a person to action of some kind, e.g. flight or fight. To enable the person to do so, an internal secretion from one of the glands is released into the bloodstream. It's effect is experienced by a feeling of breathlessness, the heartbeat speeds up, the legs may feel shaky. Athletes tell us that physical performance is greatly helped, "once they get the adrenalin going." Unfortunately, to conserve energy, other activities have to close down (clear thinking is inhibited), and what began as a simple conversation ends up in a highly charged emotional confrontation.

In such a situation, the individual should remember that the body reactions are triggered by the adrenalin, but need not be allowed to take control. Two soldiers were in battle and one of them was shaking with fright. His companion said to him, "You are scared." The other replied, "I know I am, and if you were as scared as I am, you would be running for your life." Mental control can be exercised over the physical effects, and the latter soon pass off. Panic is generated because the person does not know what to do.

To assist a person to divert the emotional effects by positive action, training is given in boat drill, first aid, life saving and road safety drill. People experienced in these schemes use up the extra energy generated by the adrenalin, by practised action.

One further effect of adrenalin is to stop the digestion for about two hours. Hence, the need to keep family quarrels and emotional scenes away from the meal table, as stated earlier.

Lack of communication is at the root of many family quarrels. Teach the lesson of Paul — talk it out, before it gets bigger. "Do not stay angry all day." (Ephesians 4:26.)

ESSENTIALS OF CHRISTIAN NURTURE 5

The Pattern Of Jesus As A Friend

Belief is the basis of what the parents live by and though children will not be able to understand about God, it is important that the parents live in faith that God is real and that we learn about Him by what he shows us of His loving nature.

For very young children, parents should begin with teaching about Jesus, for He is the image of God. They can read about Him, hear what He did and how He was the friend of all children, and in picture books and in Sunday School lessons an attempt is made to show what He *might* have looked like. Since the first pictures almost fix the impression of a person's face, care should be taken to ensure that the children see a number of different pictures of Him. Parents should say, "This is what Jesus *might* have looked like." The picture of Jesus walking with the children of all nations gives a more modern portrait. In a stained glass window in a church in Arizona, the features of Jesus have been purposely left indistinct. The artist explains that each of us carries in our heart our own portrait of the Master, and he does not wish to change that picture. The child's impression of Jesus' nature is a most important lesson, for later the child will learn that Jesus said, "Whoever has seen me has seen the Father." (John 14:9.)

The Child Goes To Church

The first stage of Christian nurture has been carried out by the parents, but it is necessary for the child to move out into the world of strangers. In the home, the child has experienced love, forgiveness, truth, but will he experience these same qualities outside? At his baptism, the congregation of his church promised to play their full part in the Christian nurture in support of the parents, and now they will be called upon to fulfil that promise.

Church provides a special group of caring people, trained and dedicated to this task, but the Sunday School does not free the congregation of its responsibility. A church of 1000 members is a church of 1000 Sunday School teachers, for good or ill every member is providing an example of Christian nurture, whenever he comes in contact with a child. As the child sits in church he is being programmed by everyone around him. Are they loving, trusting, showing him how to pray, how to worship? Does he belong to the family of God or is he just tolerated?

In his faith quest, he has absorbed the faith atmosphere of his home, at the imitative stage of development he has been influenced by the actions, moods, language of the family. Now he comes into the influence of the greater family of the church. At first, the teachers of Nursery or Beginners group are involved. They are the first strangers to have an active part in the Christian nurture, and thus the second gospel which children read is "The Acts of the Teacher in the Primary Department." The first task is the development of right relations with the children. The early experiences in the home of love, trust, forgiveness, etc. have to be made real to them in the world outside. In the family of God, this can be a vital experience. It is not so much what the teacher says, as what she is. She must be trusted and dependable, so that the home love experience can be made social. The children have to experience that those who care for them will be there for them, Sunday by Sunday, greeting them by name and though having a number of children in the class, endeavouring to establish a personal relationship with each.

ESSENTIALS OF CHRISTIAN NURTURE 6

Bible Study In The Home

The Bible is basic in Christian Education but it was not written for children. Parents and teachers have to simplify it, gradually sharing their own conviction of the importance of the lessons which it illustrates.

Bedtime

The development begins with the bedtime story routine or during the day when the child asks, "Tell me a story." Before he goes to sleep, it is helpful for parents to go over the events of the day allowing time for any hurtful events to be expressed and fears handled calmly. The child must feel safe to share experiences — happy as well as sad — with a loving, understanding parent. After the review of the day's events comes the story; sometimes an old family one or a new one, then comes a short simple prayer for Jesus' love and protection. This must not be rushed through for it is a special intimate time set apart for parent and child to be emotionally close.

Bible Stories

Early understanding of the real life basis of the Bible is important. The story is not just about the Bible characters as facts of long ago and far off places which are out of date and irrelevant, but about them as people showing a way of life to be absorbed and accepted, or to be a warning for future guidance. Human nature changes slowly. Cruelty and greed, good and evil appear and reappear time and time again. The experience of the Bible characters is still relevant, "Unless we share a little of the experience before we begin, we shall not understand what the Bible is talking about. But unless we share more of it by the time we finish, then no nurturing will actually have taken place." (*The Child in the Church*, page 29).

Other Reading/Additional Resources

As children grow in church and Sunday School, Bible study will share with worship and service in their Christian education, but some parents seem to assume that Bible study is essentially the responsibility of church and Sunday School. The success of Christian education depends on the group responsibility of all the partners in learning (school, home and church). Home Bible study in some form should underpin what is taught in Sunday School and church if it is to become real and relevant to the child's life at home. A shared 'quiet time' morning or evening with the Bible, and one of the many Bible ministries, like *Simon and Sarah, Quest, One to One* (Scripture Union) will encourage the child to discover that Bible reading is fun and relevant. Understanding the Bible as the child grows will enable a child's faith to grow also.

Parents' Example

The parents' attitude is important. If parents read the Bible and talk about it in the home, the children will conclude that it must be important and meaningful. If, however, they say that it is out of date, that it is not credible, that it cannot be true, their children will be programmed to think likewise, and the damage has been done before the church has had a chance to move. What can be ignored by parents, will be ignored by the children. If the parents are seen reading the Bible, children will want to read it too. What is real and meaningful to parents will become real and meaningful to the children.

Bible Study For Older Children

Bible study must be supported by suitable back-up materials, and a list of suitable books for parents and others is in the bibliography at the end of this booklet.

What Kind Of Book Is The Bible?

One important question which a child will ask parents is based on what is the Bible? It is a book about life and God, and it has many strands running through the various books. One such strand is that from earliest times mankind has had to face a challenge — to live with God at the centre of things, or to live as though God does not exist. In the Bible we can read the consequences of man's choice. The challenge records again and again:

"Decide today whom you will serve," says Joshua. (24:15.)

"How much longer will it take you to make up your minds?" challenges Elijah. (1 Kings 18:21.)

Jesus Reveals God

In the New Testament, God restated the challenge personally

through Jesus. "Who do you say I am?" He asks his disciples (Luke 9:20). A child must be certain, through his life experience of the home, what his parents' answer will be. But parents cannot then transfer this answer to their children. Christian nurture tells the child of the challenge, thereafter his answer is his alone. You can give them your love but not your faith.

Parents can point to another Bible truth. Jesus makes clear a target for mankind: "Seek ye first the Kingdom of God." (A.V. Matthew 6:33.) Martin Luther King found his motivation in a Vision: "I have a dream." In Proverbs 29:18 (A.V.) the same thought is expressed: "Where there is no vision the people perish." The same need is true today.

ESSENTIALS OF CHRISTIAN NURTURE 7

Teach Us To Pray

What we believe, we live by. Since we believe in God and live by faith in him, it follows naturally that we shall desire to speak to him and he to us in prayer, based on the living family situation.

Stage One

The starting point in nurture is not in what to say or when to say it. As in other learning, experience must precede instruction and so nurture begins when the child experiences parents at prayer. At first he does not know what the parents are saying but he can understand atmosphere before he can understand language. He is aware that this action seems to have great significance. By the way the parents speak of God and speak to God he comes to understand that this one they call God is a very special friend and supporter, who loves and pardons.

Gradually the child learns that the parents believe in prayer, that they live by faith and that this is part of the family pattern. Prayer, therefore, is ongoing and progressive as the child develops. Instruction can follow, based on home experience.

Stage Two

This is to teach that God hears and God acts. It is learned through stories from the Bible and other books, but also by the evident proof of family custom. By the regularity and confidence of the parents, prayer, the child tries to follow their way. Jesus said, "Ask and you will receive." (Matthew 7:7.) Parents pray in the light of that clear promise. Thus the family philosophy of divine providence is built up and consolidated.

Stage Three

As the child grows and begins to join in the family prayers, he wants to know, "Who is this that you speak to in prayer?" Parents have anticipated this question in the early years by their own attitude to God, as Father, Creator, Ruler. Each parent has his/her own way of speaking and telling about God, but what they tell reveals what they think of God, and so prayerful self-study is very important.

Stage Four

"But does God act?" After all, children have asked for many things and did not get them and so a child wonders if God acts only for adults. Here parents can assure children that God acts in all manner of ways and they can recall how God helped the family in the past. He helped, perhaps when they were ill; his guidance helped them to help others in need. Here is an ideal example of shared faith, learning together.

Answers To Prayer

Prayer is too important to be left to a once a week lesson in Sunday School. It must be introduced by parents over the years. Young children accept that their parents' lessons are true and that when they are taught to pray, do so in confidence and trust. Subsequent experience may cast doubts on the real efficiency of prayer. A Sunday School class was asked how many of them prayed, one replied, "I don't, for I've prayed for many things and I didn't get any of them." If prayers are taught, there should be some attempt to teach also that prayers *are answered* in many different ways. Four of these are important. These answers were based on how a child's own father might respond.

"Yes"

If it was for the child's own good, a loving father would grant it.

"No"

On the other hand, if a child asked his father for a sharp knife or a gun to take to school to frighten other children, father's answer would be definitely, "NO." Jesus has told us so. "And when you ask, you do not receive it, because your motives are bad; you ask for things to use for your own pleasures." (James 4:3.) Parents should make this part of Christian nurture: "If a prayer is not granted, perhaps you have not asked for the right things." How do we know what are right things? We ask all prayers, 'In Jesus' name' i.e. in accordance with what He would approve. That is why we strive to know more and more of His loving purpose, and until we know more of that purpose, we trust His will and loving care.

"Wait"

A third reply might be, "Wait, the time is not right." Adults as well as children tend to want instant satisfaction, if a prayer is not immediate they conclude that prayer does not work. Jesus advised patience — if the request is right, it will be answered in due season.

"Yes, If..."

Sometimes the answer is conditional. Many miracles of Jesus depend on this. The cripple on the mat at the Pool of Bethesda was asked, "Do you want to get well? (If you do) get up, pick up your mat and walk." (John 5:6-8.) Jesus expected a personal response first as a measure of the person's faith. So too, if a child asks his father to help in his examination, the father's answer would be, "Yes, if you prepare thoroughly first."

SOME PRACTICAL ADVICE

Believe That You Have Received The Answer

Jesus gave this promise, but we tend to limit it to what we think probable. If we have faith we praise God for what we have received in the face of not yet having received it in experience. God alone knows when everything in and around us is ready for the fulfilment of the promise, therefore faith and patience are necessary. Elijah prayed seven times for rain.

Praying For Someone Who Is Very Ill

This is a practical and common situation. Granny is ill and the child's bedtime prayer usually includes, "Bless Granny and make her better." This could be asking for the wrong thing for if Granny should die, the child's faith in prayer is challenged. The prayer should be, "Bless Granny and help the doctors and nurses to care for her and do their best for her." If the parents can augment suitable prayers, the Sunday School teacher could compile a class project book of selected prayers for the home or recommend suitable books — work books or take-home sheets which could help. It is most important in Christian nurture that prayers are based on actual home living and school experience guided by the parents. Prayer is much too important to be left to chance. But of course, "as you - - - so they." If prayer means nothing to the parent, it is not likely to mean anything to the child.

Be Definite In Prayer

Jesus asked the blind man, "What do you want me to do for you?" (Luke 18:41). The blind man had asked Jesus to have pity on him, but Jesus desired a definite request, a clear statement of the man's recognition of need. So too, in praying to be forgiven for sins, it would be better to say which sin you first want to be forgiven, and go on from there, rather than to pray for vague general absolution. Recognition of need for forgiveness is one of the first steps in praying.

The Family Prayer

The Lord's prayer was not a prayer for children, it was for his disciples; twelve men who had a desire to learn, and who were in daily contact with him. When they said, "Teach us to pray," they were asking a deeper question. (Luke 11:1.) They had no need to learn how to pray for they had been doing it all their lives, but being with Jesus at prayer they had realised that there was a new depth of prayer which they wished to share with him. If, however, the Lord's Prayer is to be taught as the Family Prayer it is important that it does not become a 'vain repetition' as William Barclay has warned. It is the pattern prayer for all prayers, and must become an essential lesson topic with repeated home support.

It begins with our vows of loyalty to God. We promise to keep His name holy; we pray that His Kingdom may come through our service; we promise to try to learn His will for we seek to do what He has intended for our good.

Thereafter, having acknowledged His sovereignty, we can then ask, *"Give us, Forgive us, Lead us, Deliver us,"* all in consequence of our affirmation of loyalty. Chanted in chorus in a Sunday School, learned 'parrot fashion,' the perfect prayer could become a ritual and not a reality.

The Prayer of Silence

"Be still and know that I am God." (A.V. Psalm 46:10.)

Most children think of prayer as speaking to God and this is true, but real communication is a two-way process involving listening as well as speaking. Michael Quoist, in his poem, "The Telephone," reminds us that prayer should be a dialogue and not a monologue.

> *'Because I didn't listen, I learned nothing,*
> *Because I didn't listen, we didn't communicate.'*

Naturally, children will find it difficult to understand silent prayer, especially if parents have not even tried it themselves, for the mind is always in motion and without something definite to concentrate on, a child's thoughts are likely to wander. But the prayer need not be long — it is the direction of the prayer that is important. "Speak Lord, I'm listening," is sufficient to open up the channel of communication. At first, it may not appear to be effective, but as the child grows, this open approach to God, in faith, can become a vital source to both child and parents.

Deeper Levels Of Prayer For Seniors

Post-primary school pupils studying the life of Jesus, can get new insight into the secrets of prayer by how he prayed. In Luke's Gospel 6:12, we read that he went out into the hills and spent all night in prayer. It is unlikely that he was speaking to God all the time — more likely, being on an intimate relationship with God, Jesus was able to draw new strength from the source of all power.

In Scripture there are many incidents of ordinary people being able to recharge their batteries, as it were, by laying themselves open to His loving care. Other religions have found this strength comes through meditation, but there is nothing new in this. The power has always been available and still is available to those who seek God in prayer.

ESSENTIALS OF CHRISTIAN NURTURE 8

Stories Of Heroes And Heroines

In past ages, the traditions of the race or clan were passed on by means of the stories of the heroes of the group. Round the camp fire and in the home, stories were told and retold, heard and re-heard and memory and imagination worked on them to keep them ever in mind but also in new forms. Children especially like stories for in the physical prowess of the hero, the child can relate his relative weakness to him. He feels he has the strength of Goliath and even today 'Superman,' or 'SuperTed' etc. continue to appeal. It is important therefore that the heroes with whom they identify, are worthy of following.

It is claimed that people are not influenced by films and TV viewing but this is not so. What we see and hear, we tend to think about; what we think about, we tend to feel in a certain way; and what we think about and feel about, we tend to do. How oft the thought of an evil deed, makes that deed done. This is inevitable for the personality is expressed in the three forces: thinking, feeling and acting. What is seen and heard must have an impact on all three. Advertisers would not spend millions of pounds on projecting their image if they thought people were not going to be influenced by TV and other media appeals. The task of the parents is to ensure that what the children see and hear are of good and kind deeds as well as having some outlet for their other tendencies. The success of a film like "Chariots of Fire" shows how the good can be as attractive as the violent or sadistic.

A teenager went into deep mourning when she learned of the death of a pop star. It took months of treatment before she could come to terms with it. The teenager was not to blame for no one had presented anyone better. Parents should ask themselves this question: "What heroes or heroines do I present in my Christian education?" Remember, if no heroes are supplied, young people will make one for themselves. The Golden Calf tendency is still as powerful as in the time of Moses.

In a Sunday School class, the teacher should endeavour to establish a personal relationship with each child. In one Sunday School a child asked the leader to pray for George. "Who is George?" she asked. "Our teacher," was the reply; "He is absent so he must be ill." Such a loving personal relationship should be the objective of all who are concerned with Christian education.

At home parents must not assume that their task of Christian nurture has now been accomplished. One hour on a Sunday could be very superficial. No parent would be satisfied if day school was limited to one hour per week. All that is taught in Sunday School has to be consolidated in the home context. If simple prayers are taught, they should be used in the home prayer. The Bible story should be told and retold, and the associated activities to the story should be continued in take-home leaflets.

Once interest has been stimulated by the teacher, extra reading material should be made available for home use. Suitable books are

'*Bible Story Time*' (Bible Reading Association), '*Story Time*' (Scripture Union), '*Bible Stories*' (Ladybird series), '*Fifty Favourite Bible Stories*' (Religion Education Press). (See also bibliography.)

To increase the development of right relationships of teacher and home, parents could encourage her to visit for tea on occasion, to let her sense the home atmosphere against which she is to frame her lesson input. Again, if the child is absent from Sunday School a telephone call or a home visit would help to assure parent and the child that the caring church acts as well as it claims to care.

ESSENTIALS OF CHRISTIAN NURTURE 9

Creative Development

When a child paints, the teacher or mother does not tell him what to draw or how to draw or what colours he has to use to paint grass, and when the picture is complete she does not criticise the artistry. She says "What a lovely picture. Tell me about it." Approval and freedom to experiment are sometimes easier to provide at playgroup than within a normal, tidy, ordered home. It is the joint activity of children playing and working together which is important, especially at the social awakening stage of 3 — 4 years.

While a child is learning to cope with his painting, adults should stand back — it is his drawing — and while he is managing, they should let him do so. Naturally a parent or teacher will stand by, repressing their innate anxiety as well as they can. Interfere only where life or limb are threatened. Activity is the means by which a child enlarges his capability. The 'good' child is the busy child — play is his work and his toys are his tools. All this is aimed at developing initiative and experiment. When a child is building bricks to make a castle, parents sometimes help and then are dismayed when he knocks it all down when the parent added the final brick. To the child, it is the creativity which is of interest and not the finished castle. Adults find difficulty in keeping their assistance to a minimum. When a child draws a man, it is his idea of a man. He may not put in the hands or legs — these will come later with closer observation and are signs of mental growth rather than artistic skill.

Indeed, drawing a man is sometimes used in early school as a test of intelligence. The famous artist Cizek whose pupils became famous, never touched up a student's work. His motto was: "To alter a child's drawing is a forgery." Helping him only emphasised his lack of ability.

The awakening to beauty is to be understood and praised. For example a young child comes into the house glowing with the sense

of achievement. "Lovely flowers mummy," she says holding out a prize bunch of flowers. One reaction would be to scold the child for picking off the heads, but the learning value of such a situation far outweighs the value of a dozen rose heads. Here is love in action, the beauty of the roses is being shared and the sense of achievement is being experienced. So mother thanks the child affectionately, mentally noting that previous experiences may not have encouraged the child to look and smell but not to take the heads off. What would she say if the child replies, "Daddy does that,". In some instances she may react negatively and angrily, but the child is not being impertinent, she is stating what she has observed previously and so mother uses the situation positively by teaching how to distinguish dead heads from buds.

As the child develops, one of the functions of art becomes more and more important. Art helps us to learn about more things, and more about things. It widens the child's horizon. Visits to new places, seeing new pictures and new buildings are all part of the child's education, but art also teaches the child to see more about things accepted as common. The poet Wordsworth says of someone, "A primrose by a river's brim, a yellow primrose was to him, and nothing more." Another poet tells how, "two men looked out from prison bars, one saw mud the other saw stars." Artistic development is an important element in personality development and faith development.

SECTION 6

SOME COMMON PROBLEMS AT HOME

Moral development in the family is concerned with the question of right and wrong behaviour. The difficulty is this: Who is to decide what is right? In some families, father decides, "It is right because I say it is," but this gives no guidance in a new situation. Morals are often a matter of geography, the use of alcohol accepted in one country can be a punishable offence in another.

Attempts have been made to lay down a set of rules of conduct e.g. the Ten Commandments, but the complexity of life brings new situations which have to be met by new laws. By the time of Jesus there were 613 rules of conduct which had to be obeyed. What was needed was a Golden Rule for general use. This Jesus provided when he answered the question, "Which is the greatest commandment in the Law?" with, "Love God and your neighbour as yourself." The working out of this Law — the Christian ethic — calls for Spiritual Development as the keystone and guide to all the other developments. Parents should make clear, in early adolescence, if there are any 'no-go areas' e.g. towards alcohol, smoking or playing golf or football at church time. Each family has its own special patterns. The young person may disregard them but he will be in no doubt as to what the parents think. It is not wise to allow a teenager to arrange a family party and then at the last minute tell the guests that they must not bring in alcohol. Parents should be clear and definite. No true sailor would venture out to sea without a chart showing rocks and shoals clearly marked. Christian nurture is a journey in life through many difficulties, some of which could be avoided by early guidance.

The Difficult Child And The Problem Of Discipline

Much of the difficulty in family life is due to lack of consistency — anything wrong one day must not be overlooked the next. Naturally, while a child is learning to adjust to living with others, he will be uncertain and will seek to see how far he will be allowed to go. Unlimited freedom is of no assistance in social learning, as in learning to drive a car, the Highway Code gives security, yet at the same time develops responsibility. Limitations are therapy, in that they define clear boundaries which are important in conserving energy which could otherwise be aimlessly misdirected.

Discipline, in some families, is deemed to limit the child's individuality, but discipline is learning and is necessary, for where everyone has liberty, no one has freedom. When a penalty has to be imposed it should be immediate, consistent and adequate as far as possible. 'Immediate' means that it should follow the offence quickly. It is not helpful to threaten that father will deal with this when he gets home, for this sets up a barrier between father and child which has no connection with the cause of the difficulty.

The Difficult Child Is A Child In Difficulty

Family and group pressure is so powerful that a child is programmed to try to please. When he is torn two ways, he is really in difficulty. It is helpful to remember that he is responding to a situation involving people, as he sees it, in the only way he has learned. Three points are involved. He is responding to a situation:

1. Involving people.

Before reacting emotionally, parents should try to find out what really happened. How did it arise? Emotion usually hinders clear thinking.

2. As he sees it.

It could be that the child is mistaken as to the situation. The teacher may not 'have a spite at him.' He may not be 'the black sheep of the family.' There may be a genuine misunderstanding. We all tend to take an incident personally, and because it's personal, we become emotional with fear or anger. Parents must hold everything and consider.

3. In the only way he has learned.

If by a wild outburst of emotion in the past he has been able to manipulate others and get his own way, he will continue to use this method until he is brought up against reality. Therapy seeks to find a better way of reacting. In such a situation, parents may say much that they regret as soon as it is uttered. In such cases, they should relax and think only of the child's difficulty. He is in a bewildering situation with parents acting out of character. A child does not understand that if a parent says, "Get out of here and don't come back," he is expressing vexation and not meaning that the loving care and support has gone. The child needs more love and care. How often have parents to forgive? In the Old Testament, the standard was three times. Jesus said that not even seventy times seven was adequate in His eyes.

The Rising Doubt

The growth of the personality can bring possible conflict of belief and attitudes which can alarm parents. The child or young person tends to want to break out, to look for proof. He is aware of double standards in those previously accepted without question, including his parents, and he asks questions. This is a matter of satisfaction to the parents, for it is a sure sign that the child's mind is being exercised critically. In such cases, parents should avoid a head-on confrontation. Often questions and doubts can open up new ways of thinking. The young person must feel safe enough to doubt, for he can rely on the steadfast support of the parents' faith and that of his church. Parents should discuss the matter calmly and if no solution is possible, agree to differ. "The church lives not only because parents pass on Christian experiences to their children, but because parents and children share new Christian experiences which can be interpreted in the light of the tradition. The tradition itself is renewed in the process." The level of faith of the parents will not be copied exactly. What the parents pass on is the ability to think through to appropriate action which is emotionally satisfying. "In Christian nurture the uncertainty of doubt is replaced by the uncertainty of faith." ('*The Child in the Church*,' Page 24, British Council of Churches).

The Rebel

Parents generally watch the early stages of child development — physical growth milestones are deemed to be important — but once the child goes to school, the anxieties of the early days seem less important. "Were we wrong to worry about his sleep pattern?" "Why did we worry because he was slow in toilet training?" One factor, however, which many parents fail to notice, is that he is maturing and becoming independent. Father sometimes cannot tell on the spur of the moment, "Is your son 15 or 16?" In a two-parent family with two or more children, a steady routine with much involvement in youth organisations enables the young person to mature almost unnoticed, except perhaps for his physical development. It comes as a shock, therefore, to be reminded of the rebel which lies beneath the surface of even the most obedient children. The shock is all the greater since the parents have assumed that there cannot be smoke without fire. In most cases there is no specific cause which can be pointed out; the pressure has been building up as maturation grew and one small incident has been sufficient to bring things out into the open.

A frequent complaint of parents is to ask, "How could he do this to us, after all that we have done for him?" A young person may not look at it in this way; he feels the pressure is on his self-development and his self-esteem and his reaction is personal to himself just as their reaction is personal to them. His unspoken reply could be, "After all these years, do you really think that I would do something silly?" Further questioning usually is met by a

blank stare of defiance. The shutters have come down on both sides. Parents hardly recognise their own child.

A rebel is sustained by the emotional energy created by the pressure (actual or implied) from the parents or a situation at school or outside. The first step, therefore, is to avoid a similar emotional reaction. Naturally it is disturbing because it is usually so unexpected but parents should be glad to see the growth of independence, and rather than attempt to repress the new urge they should try to redirect the new energy as calmly as possible. If the young person has been nurtured in love and faith thus far, there is every chance that the life pattern built in by the home will determine the outcome. Children in rebellion often say things which are very hurtful and unjust e.g. "I feel stifled," "You don't like my friends," "You are always getting on to me." One teenager put it, "You would not get peace to die in this house."

Parents are tempted to say, "We didn't do that sort of thing in our day," but this has no relevance to the discussion and, moreover, such a theme tends to side-track the parents into a hopeless position. After all, the value of money, forms of entertainment, music to enjoy, have all changed. But parents can show that the moral values of the past are still valid today, and that their love, their support and their trust still stands. The prodigal son's father did not run after him or try to dissuade him from going. He was content that he had provided the safe base camp from which his son was keen to move and to which he could return. The door was always open, for love is not love if it is conditional on behaviour.

School refusal is one difficulty which upsets many parents. Modern regimes in primary schools are so relaxed that truancy is not general. Change of school can cause a problem. Transfer from a small school in the country to a large town school can be a cause of anxiety, but need not become acute so long as the parents do not contribute to the emotional climate. After all, most people have situations when they would rather stay at home than go out and children are just as likely to prefer to play with a train-set or pet rabbit.

The quicker the situation is handled, the less likely it is to become a habit. As in industrial relations, the rule should be, "back to work, pending investigations." Almost always there are no signs of illness though the child may complain of aches and pains or sickness which disappears when it is past nine o'clock, at the weekend or during the holidays. Naturally, in such instances, a medical check would be essential and the rare cases treated, but in the majority of situations there is no real medical problem.

In many cases the child is manipulating his environment. Two explanations are suggested. The child may feel he is in complete control of his environment and refuses to go, because nobody can make him or he is so timid and afraid of the new school situation that he cannot cope for the present. The school psychological service in co-operation with school and parents should be able to suggest the remedy. It is imperative for the child's future happiness that he learns to face up to his difficulties for only he can solve the difficulty.

The abolition of corporal punishment at home and in schools marked a considerable change in discipline but it did not meet the problem of bullying. A recent report states, "Almost every child, even many girls, have to meet this at some time or another, and the school tradition against clyping makes it difficult to control."

The main solution is for the school to be vigilant and known to be so. It is to be made clear to every child that bullying will not be tolerated. It will persist, however, so long as the bully is enjoying his power over the victim. Once it is faced, the power and enjoyment begin to disappear. The problem is so severe and so difficult to detect that a study booklet has been produced by Strathclyde Regional Council, and is available to all schools.

In addition to vigilance, the school should encourage the senior pupils to have a role of unobtrusive caring as well as setting a good example. They must be aware of what is going on beneath the surface.

Parents too have a part to play. It is fatal to do nothing. Though they may not be encouraged to complain, it is essential that they alert the staff to the need for action. The good name of the school is important, but must not be protected if the situation demands that it be known and is being dealt with timeously.

Frustration

One of the great gifts which parents can bestow on their children is to teach them how to deal with frustration. All through life, but especially in childhood, frustration will be a common experience. A very young child, faced with a closed door which he cannot open usually reacts by an emotional outburst, kicking the door, crying in despair, screaming with rage — all equally unavailing but upsetting to the parents, especially if strangers or relatives are disapproving. Without getting equally emotional, parents should treat such a situation as a great opportunity for teaching patience and control of emotion. The child has to learn from repeated experiences that wild outbursts of anger will not have any effect on doors or any other object and it does not take long for this life-lesson to be absorbed. Unfortunately, a child soon discovers that parents can be manipulated by emotional scenes and demands, and if this succeeds the pattern tends to be reinforced and can become a habit in adulthood. "The child is father of the man."

Training starts with calm non-emotional reaction of the parents. Patiently show the positive way to meet frustration, e.g. with the closed door incident.

1. Show the child how to turn the handle in the correct way and then get him to do it himself. If it is a key which is proving difficult, more force can make matters worse.

2. If he is too small, show him how to reach the handle by using a small stool.

3. Teach the child to look for another way. Frustration tends to make a small incident become one of major importance. Pre-school play material, e.g. posting box and inset boards are specially valuable for this. Mother shows that if a block will not fit one space, emotion or hammering will not solve the problem, but that he should try another space or a different block. In time, the method becomes established that there is usually another way round a difficulty. Positive thinking is one of the aims in Christian nurture.

The Problem Of Jealousy

One common form in which frustration is found is jealousy. Since each person has a self-image, anything which seems to diminish that may well be resented. In families, sibling rivalry can be anticipated if one child seems to be preferred to another because he is the only boy among sisters; the only girl among brothers; the clever one in the family; the less able in the family. Parents are often guilty of comparing one child with another, but it may be that there has been no actual discrimination, and that the child is misreading the situation.

There are many occasions when displacement has occurred. The new baby inevitably involves an older child in some loss of attention from mother and from visitors eager to see the new baby. Reassurance to the older child that he is still loved, has little effect, for he has lost his unique place to the newcomer. With patience and understanding the child has to discover through experience that he has not lost his place in the family. He finds that he can be quite secure and that instead of getting a rival he is actually having a new playmate who is *his* baby as well as mother's baby. Every effort should be made to include him in talks about the baby, in helping with feeding and bathing *his* brother or sister. Relatives visiting must be prepared to meet his need for some notice, especially if formerly he was the centre of attraction. After the baby has been put to bed, mother should try to restore the balance by having a specially close link through a story, game or special interest. In her anxiety or stress of bringing up a new baby, mother may overlook the loss of place and father could help by more personal attention. Fortunately in most families, jealousy fades as the exclusive attention of the mother becomes less and less as the baby grows.

Learning Through Involvement In The Church

The objective in Christian education is not merely to teach Bible truths but to enable our young people to learn how to live in fellowship and service in obedience to those truths. They learn this through meeting together for worship but such a group is not necessarily a fellowship. There has to be a feeling of belonging, of being actively involved with others in the structure, sharing in the planning and direction. Unfortunately in a large congregation scope is limited by the number of people who can become actively involved in other then worship and finance. It always seems that the same people are in everything and others have to be content in the pews. This is specially true of teenagers and may in part explain their absence from a normal service. A writer has suggested recently that, "young people are a forgotten mission field today." Parents can have great influence on the degree of involvement of their young people. With patience yet also with encouragement, young people tend to accept the parents' guidance so long as they do not feel that they are under pressure or 'being got at.' If, however, the parents are merely adherents, their young people will feel no call to a fellowship whose evangelism lacks conviction.

Young people attract young people, and so parents should encourage any form of youth group in the church and provide encouragement and practical assistance, including finance. Sunday School, Bible Class, Youth Fellowship and Choir offer opportunities for service, but these do not take account of the diversity of interests and talents of those outside the church. The problem will be to provide opportunity to other groups to become involved in worthwhile types of service, and not just menial 'maintenance-orientated' tasks which no one else will perform, for such gratuitous opportunities create indifference, or worse, resentment.

The Spirit Of A Place

Appreciation of and response to the spirit of a place is an important element in Christian nurture. From time to time, and not just for the opening worship, the children should be in church to enable them to experience this input of the spirit of the place, and to be able to react to the worship of the congregation. They may not understand the words of the anthem or hymn but experience of worship should not be neglected. We tend to emphasise the need to understand, and play down the emotional impact of worship in fellowship with others.

The spirit of a place is important in itself and so the children should visit the church when it is empty and let them feel more at ease. Usually they sit in one part and go in and out without being aware of the message of the building itself. If however, they go round

and are told the story of the windows and furnishings, about the symbols of the pulpit fall and other items, they could identify with them, and when visiting other churches begin to look with understanding at the "message all mankind may use, and most refuse". After all, the symbols and windows were not merely for decoration; each was put there as an aid to worship. Sometimes all is not at once obvious and clear, but the windows were designed for prayerful study for the present congregation and the children of tomorrow.

Such a visit of discovery would be valuable as home take-back material for most of the congregation sit in the same seats Sunday by Sunday, and parents especially, are often unaware of the impact of the whole building, the richness of the symbolism, the heritage from past generations of people at worship.

This spirit of a place was vividly illustrated in the following incident. A member of a visiting seaside mission team who had come merely to get a holiday but did not want to take part in the mission, found that the day to day contact with the empty church, and the morning and evening worship in it, brought a strange sense of the spirit of the place. He began to join in the worship as a totally new experience. As he said, he felt that the spirit of the hundreds of

55

people of the past, their prayers and their praises had somehow transformed a mere building into a sanctuary, and there and then he determined to join wholeheartedly in the mission project. At the closing service, he spoke movingly of his experience of the fellowship of the team, but especially of the change the building itself had made on his whole attitude to things.

The spirit of a place depends also on the people in it. A church is a fellowship of believers who show concern for others. A young child attending a church asked "Why are all the people smiling as they come in?" "Because they have been welcomed at the door and are sure that they will be made welcome by those inside."

The vigour and enthusiasm of young people for life and adventure has to find a cause with which they can identify. The ideal of a brave world won for righteousness does appeal to youth, but young people will not accept that ideal nor the sacrifices which it demands if they are merely tolerated or kept inactive 'below-decks' until they are mature enough to join the church. Parents who have nurtured their young people thus far, must encourage their church to seek and plan new outreach to them. Their enthusiasm and idealism are needed in the church, and could bring fresh insight into the worship and service.

Four Special Experiences

In Christian education four experiences are especially valuable as learning situations.

1. **Baptism.** On occasion, parents and children will be present at a baptism. What this will mean to the parents will tend to mean to the children at their level of understanding. If baptism is merely a tradition to give the child a name, they will fail to understand the importance of God's involvement in it. He has called the child to become a member of His family and is surrounding him with His grace. Parents can pass on only what they know and feel about it. It is in no way a 'Christening.'

2. **Marriage.** When parents and children attend a wedding ceremony, both can share some insight into the importance of marriage. Two people who have been independent personalities thus

far, are pledging themselves to a unique relationship of love and trust, the stability of which will determine the endurance and quality of the Christian nurture of their children. So many children and parents are being programmed to regard marriage as a temporary relationship. Christian nurture teaches the Christian view of marriage: it is a commitment and not an experiment.

3. **Youth Camp.** A most invaluable experience for young people is to attend a church Youth Camp, a Summer School, an S.U. Camp, or similar 'Retreat.' There is such a flow of fellowship, a new vision of the familiar routine, that young people, beginning to feel dissatisfied and isolated by the older members, suddenly discover that worship in a new environment and within a new fellowship becomes more real and more relevant. The talks, the inspiring leadership, and the discussion groups, often going on long into the night, all contribute to what for some is almost a conversion experience. In many camps, young people come back for several years building on their new view of things and all come home to their church invigorated and strengthened in their faith.

4. **Holy Communion.** The child's understanding of the Lord's Supper is similarly programmed by early experience of the parents' attitude to communion. Other churches, e.g. Orthodox Church, have realised the importance of nurture within the church. There, children are Baptised, Confirmed or admitted to First Communion at the age of a few months. Thereafter, they are nurtured in the church and move from infancy to adult membership without interruption.

The Value Of A Worth While Youth Organisation

It is often asked, "Do youth organisations make children good? Or are 'good' children mainly from supportive homes?"

There is no doubt that both are true, but the value of a code of accepted behaviour does help in the upbuilding of useful habits of behaviour i.e. service to others and a high standard of what is right.

The Francis Report (1984) surveyed 1300 church-going young

people of all denominations in England. It found that 60% of them would like to see their churches give more time to helping local people and that they would want to be involved in such a program. 52% wanted more opportunity to share their thoughts with each other in a Christian context. Is the church prepared to listen to what our young people are saying?

SECTION 7

CHILDREN AT COMMUNION

The recent approval by the General Assembly for the admission of children to Communion rejected eight years ago but again to be referred to Presbyteries and Kirk Sessions, calls for a careful examination of the present position. In the Church of Scotland there is a clear barrier to real membership. Confirmation and Communion have become linked. The Church Family at Communion is a family without children. Compare this with the practice in other denominations. In the Roman Catholic Church, children are instructed in the significance of Communion, and take their First Communion about the age of 7 years. This is a unique family occasion and friends and relatives are invited to celebrate the new relationship of child and Church. The child is nurtured in the Church fellowship. The Church of England admits children by about 12—13 but it is open to parents to take responsibility for earlier ability to participate. Again they are nurtured in the Church fellowship. In the Church of Scotland the children are nurtured by the Church. At baptism parents take vows that they will nurture their children in the faith, but are given little clear guidance as to how this can be carried out. Congregations too are enjoined to assist parents in Christian nurture, but again no specific advice is provided.

The task is given to the Sunday School staff to lead the children through Creche, Beginners and Primary Departments, Junior and Senior Sunday School, and finally Bible Class. Thereafter, just when the children are ready to move forward into the deeper fellowship and service of the Church, they are left with little encouragement or further instruction until they are judged to be able to take vows of Membership and so qualify to attend Communion. The Sacrament should not be regarded as a sign of grace — it is really a means of grace enabling them to grow spiritually to more mature Christians. If it is claimed that they would not understand what they are doing, how many of the adults understand what they are doing? Despite the fact that elders visit every member, and issue invitation cards and these cards are then counted to check the attendances, many members fail to attend Communion even once a year.

THE IMPORTANCE OF PARENTAL INVOLVEMENT

The request for children to be admitted to Communion should therefore come mainly from the parents. They must convince the Church that they understand its importance and they desire to extend the Christian nurture of the Sunday School and Bible Class.

The Elder Calls

The early lesson begins when the elder calls at Communion time. Ideally, he/she shall have become a friend of the family having visited at important events, but the Communion time may be the first opportunity for actual learning, when someone from the Church, called an elder, visits, and leaves a 'card'. Who is this person? Why does he/she visit? Why is a 'card' left each time? Children learn by asking questions. Instead of sending the children out to play, therefore, they should be encouraged to meet the elder so that a personal link may be established. "Mr. A or Mrs. B, a friend of the family has come to assure us that the Church cares for its members and brings news of the various Church activities. In order to keep contact, a 'card' invites us to a special service. Very soon we hope that you will be able to come with us." Show the card. "You see it has our name on it and also Mr. A's or Mrs. B's name." If the child can read, ask him to tell you what it says. 'In remembrance of me?' 'Who do you think is *me*?' Though the card is from the Church, who is really inviting us to come?"

Parents' Reaction

The second informal lesson which is often overlooked comes from the parents' response to the visit. Has the house been tidied up? Has father put on a clean pullover? Is the elder left at the door and not invited to meet the family? Has father reluctantly turned off the TV and disappeared from the room as the elder comes to the door? Do the family continue to watch the TV while the elder is speaking of the church? Is the conversation all about football or politics? (All very friendly, but not relevant to the reason for the visit.) All these are important signs to the child. He sees, he hears, he thinks, he learns, he is being programmed about the parents' view of elders, visits, Communion.

The Result Of The Visit

Important, too, is the outcome of the visit. What do the parents say after the elder has left? Are the cards put away in a drawer with the previous cards? Do the parents go to the services? If nothing happens, the child concludes that Communion, and the elder's visitations have no relevance. Do the parents attend the services but leave the children still asleep at home? (At least Sunday School and Bible Class should not be cancelled on Communion Sundays.)

Parents' Negative Signals

Throughout, stress is laid on the informal lesson of the parents' precept and example — especially the negative signals. If the sacrament is felt to be a mournful occasion, if parents attend from a sense of duty but complain of the length or content of the sermon afterwards, these negative signals will be picked up by the children. If, however, parents show that the symbols, words and actions of the sacrament arouse thoughtful remembrance of all Jesus has done for the world, they will come from the service strengthened by his presence and the warm fellowship of the people, to go forward into the future in faith and joy.

The Need For Positive Action By Parents

If children see neighbours going to Communion while their own parents stay at home they must wonder if it is only for certain people but not for them. If, however, parents establish that Communion is part of the family pattern, the child growing up in this family naturally expects to go, just as he goes elsewhere with them. Experience precedes instruction.

We can learn much from the way in which Jewish children learn about the passover. When the table has been set, the younger son asks his father, "Why did the Lord our God command us to obey all these laws?" (Deuteronomy 6:20.) The father then explains the origin and significance of the sacrament. The fact that the child asks the question shows that he sees himself as part of the community of faith. Through a combination of words, visual signs and actions — sharing the meal — the child participates in and is nurtured in the faith of the family and the community to which he belongs.

A similar line of thought could apply to our own children so that when the time comes they can take upon themselves the vows made on their behalf.

Parents cannot make clear to their children what is not clear to themselves. It is urgent, therefore, that they look closely at their own view of communion. Why is it so important? Parents should be aware of five aspects:

1. Divine Institution

The sacrament of the Lord's Supper was commended by Jesus himself; "Do this in memory of me." (1 Corinthians 11:24.) It is therefore a divine command to all who claim to accept him as Lord and Saviour. He instituted this sacrament because He was about to leave his disciples and deeply desired to leave important practical instructions for them to pass on to others in the future.

2. Divine Presence

Though Jesus is always near, we believe and have found from experience that He is truly present with us at communion. As we sing, "Here, oh my Lord, I see thee face to face," we 'remember' Him, not as a mere memory of someone long since dead, but in 're-living,' re-enacting the experience of the disciples. Through the power of the Holy Spirit the 'there and then' of their experience becomes the 'here and now' of our own experience.

3. Divine Hope

At every communion we affirm our belief and hope for the future for we "proclaim the Lord's death until He comes." (1 Corinthians 11:26.)

4. Belonging

The success in Christian upbringing is not measured only by scripture knowledge. Of great importance is the quality of personal relationships which a child forms with other people. Without help from adults, children tend to keep to their own peer group, but by worshipping with adults, the joy of fellowship can begin to be experienced.

Mere attendance with others is not enough, there must be active involvement, the greatest source of the feeling of belonging comes from sitting together at a fellowship meal at communion. There they can begin to realise what it means to belong to the family of God. They grow in interest and in confidence when they feel that they belong.

5. Thanksgiving

One of the terms for communion is eucharist, i.e. thanksgiving, and this can be meaningful for children if home training has given opportunity for expressing it. The child who learns to thank, to say "Sorry," or, "Please," to those whom he has seen at home is much more likely to wish to give thanks to God or express regret for wrongdoing. In this respect good manners is good Christian nurture.

At communion we give thanks for all that Christ has done for us. Most Christians are only too aware of their own short comings. As Paul has said, "All have sinned, but we are redeemed sinners through Christ's sacrifice." (Romans 3:22-26.) Thanksgiving and repentance, therefore, is our due response.

When Is A Child Ready For Communion?

This is a perennial query in all growth. When should he be able to talk, or walk, or sleep through the night? There is no set age marking development. In school it is merely for convenience that a child starts at age five. Some five-year-olds are not ready for schooling, but have to go; some four-year-olds are ready to go, but cannot. By secondary school age children should be able to make a start by being present at a communion service accompanied by a parent or teacher. After the service the parent should talk about the very special day when an important milestone has been passed. The service marks the first major step of growing up in the church. Any misunderstandings, inevitable in youth, will be corrected within the fellowship at subsequent communions. The children will be nurtured *in* the church, rather than *by* the church.

When a young person is finally admitted to Communion, great insight at first is not called for. Here, the support of the whole congregation is important, for he comes within the all-surrounding movement of God's grace promised to him and his parents at his baptism. The congregation's pledge to assist in his nurture can now be of vital importance; he has come of age.

SOME SUGGESTIONS ON CONSIDERING A COMMUNION SERVICE WITH CHILDREN

1. Since the idea is new and difficult, clear guidelines and experiments are essential.
2. There is no question of marching the Sunday School 'en masse' to Communion. It is a personal family commitment, shared with the parents and congregation. The children will sit with their parents and in the early stages of the experiment, children will be of secondary school age.
3. Special pre-Communion instruction will be provided by Bible Class leaders or senior Sunday School teachers, under the direction of the minister.

4. Any change will be permissive and no congregation will be forced to admit children against its will. Full discussion will be made by the Kirk Session regarding seating, time of sermon and procedure (e.g. is wine to be used?)

5. As part of the instruction, opportunity will be taken to enable children to be present at a Communion to become familiar with the order of service.

6. Congregations may require to be convinced of the need to nurture children through to full membership. A Church family without children is incomplete.

7. When elders visit at Communion times, opportunity should be taken to speak to parents on the need to think seriously of their children being considered for instruction.

8. After instruction, baptised children should be eligible for admission to the Communion Roll by the Kirk Session at the request of the parents and a Profession of Faith suitable to the child's understanding.

CONCLUSION

From Cradle Roll to Communion Roll is one of the objects of Christian parenting. To lay the foundations on which parents and children can build is an important duty for parents to promise to undertake. Parents are not left to do this on their own. The Holy Spirit enables them to undertake this task.

The above picture shows two windows depicting Solomon dedicating the temple and the disciples being sent out. This helps us to remember that we come as a family into church to worship in order that we can go out in service. We can only achieve this through the cross bringing the two together. The risen Lord enables us to go out into all the world to preach the gospel in the power of the Holy Spirit. "We gather for worship in order to scatter for service."

BIBLIOGRAPHY

BIBLE

The Bible Story (series 1-8) (National Christian Education Council)
Introducing the Bible Barclay (International Bible Reading Association)
Fount Children's Bible   (Collins)
Bible Commentary   Neil   (Hodder and Stoughton)
Companion to the New Testament Harvey   (Cambridge University Press)
Oxford Bible Atlas   (Oxford University Press)
Bible Readers' Encyclopedia and Concordance Clow (Collins)
Ethics in a Permissive Society Barclay (Collins-Fontana) 1971

PRAYER

Prayers to use with 11-13s,   (N.C.E.C)
Prayers to use with young people,   (N.C.E.C.)
When you pray with _ _ _ _, (Series 3-6, 7-10s) (N.C.E.C)
With Christ in the School of Prayer, Murray (Fleming Ravell Co.) 1976
Prayers for Younger People, Barclay   (Collins) 1963

CHILD STUDY

Onward Christian Parents, Copley (Church House) 1986
What do we really want for our children?, Sharp (Epworth) 1986
The Child in the Church, (British Council of Churches) 1984
Bringing up Children in the Christian Faith, Westerhoff III (Winston) 1980
Children — the Challenge to the Church, Hamilton (Church of Scotland)
Christian Child Development, Iris Cully (Gill and Macmillan)
New Ground in Christian Education, Loukes (S.C.M.) 1965
Positive Teaching, Wheldall and Merrett (Unwin) 1984
Psychology and You, Berryman et al. (B.P.S. Methuen) 1987
The Needs of Children, (Keller Pringle) 1986
Memory, Thinking and Language, (Judith Greene) 1987

Learning to Think, (Open University Course) 1991
Calling all Parents, Duncan (St. Andrew Press, Third Edition) 1978
Startlers for Parents, Duncan (St. Andrew Press) 1978
Praying with Children, Duncan (St. Andrew Press) 1980
How Shall we Care, Duncan (St. Andrew Press) 1986
Children at The Table, (Hamilton & MacDonald) 1982
Working with Children and Their Families, Herbert (British Psychology Society) 1988
A Faith for the Year 2000, Roy Paterson (St Andrew Press) 1990
Teenagers and the Church, L Francis (Collins) 1981